Benevolent Magic
&
Living Prayer

*Ancient Secrets
of
Feminine Science*

Reveals the Mysteries through Robert Shapiro

BOOKS BY ROBERT SHAPIRO

Explorer Race series

1. The Explorer Race
2. ETs and the Explorer Race
3. Explorer Race: Origins and the Next 50 Years
4. Explorer Race: Creators and Friends
5. Explorer Race: Particle Personalities
6. The Explorer Race and Beyond
7. Explorer Race: The Council of Creators
8. The Explorer Race and Isis
9. The Explorer Race and Jesus
10. Explorer Race: Earth History and Lost Civilizations
11. Explorer Race: ET Visitors Speak
12. Explorer Race: Techniques for Generating Safety

Material Mastery series

A: Shamanic Secrets for Material Mastery
B: Shamanic Secrets for Physical Mastery
C: Shamanic Secrets for Spiritual Mastery

Shining the Light series

Ultimate UFO series

Secrets of Feminine Science series

Benevolent Magic
&
Living Prayer

Ancient Secrets
of
Feminine Science

Reveals the Mysteries through Robert Shapiro

ॐ Light Technology Publishing

ISBN 1-891824-49-X

Published by

Light Technology Publishing
PO Box 3540
Flagstaff, AZ 68003
1-800-450-0985
www.lighttechnology.com

Printed by

GraphTech
DIGITAL & PRINTING

4030 E. Huntington Dr.
Flagstaff, AZ 86004
1-928-526-1345

INTRODUCTION

Benevolent magic can only be used benevolently, even if it is accidentally (or otherwise) said in some way that isn't benevolent. It will still only work as long as the experience for everyone is benevolent, including those who cooperate consciously or otherwise with bringing about your request.

Benevolent magic is a request, not just words. Many of you will feel energy after you say the request. The fundamentals of benevolent magic are what you say and how you say it. Benevolent magic is provided by loving beings to help allow you and train you as a global community to begin doing things that will support each and every one of you.

TABLE OF CONTENTS

1

BENEVOLENT MAGIC AND LIVING PRAYER: USE FEMININE SCIENCE TO CHANGE YOUR WORLD

Reveals the Mysteries
November 21, 2004

Benevolent magic is a system designed to go beyond what you now know as prayer. Prayer is a system because it clearly defines what you want and need for yourself, your family, your friends, your community—the world. And it does so in a structured way that allows you to feel connected to Creator, whoever or whatever that named identity for Creator in your religion or philosophy is. Benevolent magic is a little different. It doesn't replace any of that prayer that you now do—continue to do that as you like. But it supports that.

Benevolent magic is separate in that it works directly with Creator, angels and benevolent beings, and the benevolent portion of the souls of all beings on Earth and everywhere. It can only be used benevolently, even if it is accidentally (or otherwise) said in some way that isn't benevolent. It will still only work as long as the experience for everyone is benevolent, including those who cooperate consciously or otherwise with bringing about your request . . . that's the whole point.

Benevolent Magic Allows a Sense of Union with All Beings

Benevolent magic is a request, not just words. Many of you will feel energy after you say the request. Sit with the energy if you can or feel the energy—not necessarily if you're operating a automobile, but let the energy be there if it possibly can be. It will fade or lessen, to a degree, in most cases.

Now, many times you won't feel any energy. Then just go on after you complete it. Benevolent magic is provided by loving beings to help allow you and train you as a global community to begin doing things that will support each and every one of you. I know that you all want a cooperative, benevolent global community where everybody has what they need and everybody has the opportunity to have what they want.

Benevolent magic is intended, then, to allow you to cooperate in some way with other people who ask for something that cooperation on your part might help to provide—even though you won't know who they are or what they ask (maybe they're on the other side of the world). Your cooperation might be some tiny little thing that you will do unconsciously. It doesn't have control or power over you.

It might just mean that instead of scratching your head, you scratch your arm. It might be something silly like that, which may seem to be totally trivial and inconsequential but that could have some subtle effect. I am trying to suggest, then, that it would not be something that commands or overtakes your life, but it will allow you to make some trivial change in your life that will not harm you in any way.

The reason benevolent magic works is that all souls, all beings, who cooperate to help bring about in some way a benevolent result (also known as a benevolent outcome for your benevolent magic that you say and request) must be doing only something—if it's something different that they do at all—that is completely benevolent for them. So no one suffers in any way. Things just shift and change gently.

So this is training for you. I know that many of you have tried to find a philosophy, a governmental system, a way of thinking, a way of feeling—all kinds of different things—that everyone can feel good about and that will work for everyone. This system of benevolent magic may not be a government system; it may not be a religion. But it may have some aspects that suggest that it is a portion of some philosophy, perhaps, or that it can fit into a great many philosophies. It is not intended to replace the family system, friends or relationships.

This is not intended to replace medical science or anything like that. But it is intended to allow you to have a means by which you can cooperate with all other beings in a way that's totally benevolent for you. And just on that alone, it is a good system that will begin, gently, to allow you to have a sense of union with all beings.

The Fundamentals of Benevolent Magic

The fundamentals of benevolent magic are what you say and how you say it. I will now give an example of benevolent magic: You might say, "I request that I experience a most benevolent interview for my new job, and that that job will bring about a most benevolent outcome for me." That would be an example of a benevolent-magic statement.

You can tell, just by that statement, that it really sounds like something you might reasonably say to anyone. It might even be incorporated in a prayer or a request that you've made at other times. But it will have effects, and they will all be only benevolent.

I know I'm saying the word "benevolent" a lot, but I'm trying to underscore this because the word "magic" is in the title, and many of you have all kinds of ideas about what magic is. Magic, granted, appears to have something to do with that man or woman on the stage (or a youngster perhaps) who magically pulls something out of a hat, and you have no idea how that got in there. Or that person pours a glass of milk into the hat and then taps the hat and apparently . . . where'd the milk go? So that seems to be magic as well. Then you've heard of magic that is kind of frightening and scary, and then also magic that compensates for that, which is gentle and loving and makes everything fine. So the term "benevolent magic" is the factor here. That's why I'm explaining this a bit.

The function of benevolent magic does not really work very well unless you say it. It is not something that you say only for powerful and important moments in your life, such as the new job. You can also say it for the simplest little things, meaning . . . say you're going to go to have a hair appointment, get your hair done or maybe just get a haircut. So you might say, "I request that my appointment at the hair salon"—"or at the barber"—"go completely benevolently for me today, including a wonderful parking spot right out in front, and that this result in the most benevolent outcome for me."

Benevolent Magic

"I request that my appointment at the hair salon go completely benevolently for me today, including a wonderful parking spot right out in front, and that this result in the most benevolent outcome for me."

Benevolent Outcomes That Involve Others

Now, there will be times when you will say something where the request for the benevolent outcome might involve other people. For instance, you might say, "I request that my family outing today with everybody go well and smoothly for me, and that I experience at this outing great benevolence and happiness, and that this result in a most benevolent outcome."

> *Benevolent Magic*
>
> *"I request that my family outing today with everybody go well and smoothly for me, and that I experience at this outing great benevolence and happiness, and that this result in a most benevolent outcome."*

In this case, at the end we don't say "for me," because it's something you're doing with others—in this case, others whom you care about. In that case, unless you get a strong feeling at the end—by strong I mean something that you really feel uncomfortable about and you find that if you say "for me," that that works better—then good, but if you don't get that feeling, then just say "benevolent outcome," period, because it involves others directly.

For those of you who have an office or a business, you might say something similar: "That new project we're starting today," for instance, like that. Say, "I request that our new project at the office that we're beginning today go well and smoothly for me, and that all of the aspects of it fit very benevolently into place, and that this result in a most benevolent outcome," period. There are lots of other people at the office, and perhaps the project will result in some product that you hope will go out and serve the greater community and support your office and your business to produce other good products. So say, "the most benevolent outcome," period, because other people are involved.

That's not a hard and fast rule, but I'm telling it to you like that because many of you who are reading this book have not had a great deal of experience with things like this. So I'm suggesting this as a working rule. That is my suggestion along those lines.

Benevolent Magic

"I request that our new project at the office that we're beginning today go well and smoothly for me, and that all of the aspects of it fit very benevolently into place, and that this result in a most benevolent outcome."

Try to Say It Out Loud

Now, there are other situations with benevolent magic when benevolent magic requires from you a moment to pause, meaning that you are doing something. Perhaps you're at work and you really need to do something; you feel the urgent need to say benevolent magic about something. If you're in the middle of something, you can say it under your breath, so to speak.

But try to say it at least out loud—whispering is out loud—because this is a change you want to affect your physical world for you. Therefore, for your body to know and understand that this is physical (and your body is deeply involved in the creation of your physical world and experience), it needs to be physicalized. Thinking it may not work very well. In most cases, it won't work at all, but in some cases, it might work a little bit. So try to at least whisper it. You can whisper it softly, but that's what I recommend.

Say Benevolent Magic for Yourself, Say Living Prayer for Others

I know you want the world to be a better place and everybody to be happy and get along cooperatively.

But we do not say benevolent magic directly for others, and I'll tell you why. Benevolent magic is very influential, and it doesn't require a lot from people, most of whom you don't know and will never meet—maybe just a tiny little gesture or a little move, a little something different than they would've done that is perfectly all right with them to do that way. This is something insignificant for most people. But in the case of benevolent magic, eventually it is quite a significant outcome for you.

So we don't say benevolent magic for others because we have to allow them to choose to say it for themselves. However, there is something we can say for others, and this is something that will sound very similar to things you have already done. I will touch on that in this book.

Although this book is primarily geared toward benevolent magic, I want to touch a little bit on living prayer. Living prayer is the form of benevolent magic that you can say when you really feel the need—or even if you gently feel the need—to say something for someone else specifically, even if that person wouldn't think to say it for himself, wouldn't want to say it for himself or, as is much more often the case, doesn't know how to say it for himself.

Say you hear about something on the news—this comes up a lot. You are watching a news program and they say somewhere on the other side of the world that there's been a terrible earthquake and they don't know what's happening, but they'll give you more updates and so on. They mention the name of the location where it is, and you want to do something and you would be happy to make a contribution of some sort, but the news people don't even know what it is and you feel frustrated and upset because you want to do something immediately to serve that. That's where living prayer comes in.

I will give you an example, and I will mention the name of a country where you have heard of earthquakes before. Of course, you have them right here in the United States, but there are other countries that have earthquakes, sometimes even more often than you have them, so I will use another country as an example. You might say a living prayer because you're saying something for others who don't know about it, who don't know how to say it, who might not think to say it or who might be in a dire emergency where someone will have to say something else for them because they are in desperate straits, possibly in pain, and all they can say, if they can say anything at all, is to just beg for help. And if they're doing that, you can help to bring it about.

This is what you might say; I will give you an example directly. You might say—don't say, "I request"— "I am asking that all the people in Japan," and you mention the name of the place if you know it. If you don't know the name of the place, meaning specifically, then just say the name of the country—you'll remember that. Then say, "who are suffering and need help"—you don't necessarily have to say "who are suffering," but I'm mentioning it in this case—"receive all the help and support and love that they need from all those beings who can help them."

Living Prayer

"I am asking that all the people in _____ who are suffering and need help receive all the help and support and love that they need from all those beings who can help them."

Now, there's a reason I say "beings." You might say, "Well, why don't you just say 'people'?" Well, because there are times when it won't just be human beings. You've all seen on the news where dogs go in and try to find people in an earthquake. You've also had in your thoughts and imaginations that maybe somebody is in pain and human beings won't be able to get that person out in time and maybe it would comfort her to have angels and spirits and Creator and God to come to her.

Even though you know and believe that God and the angels will come anyway, this is a way you can speak for that person. It will help you to feel better because you are doing something, and it will also, if people can be rescued—which very often they can— support and nurture and encourage that support to come to those people as quickly as possible.

With Living Prayer, the Outcome Will Be Benevolent

You might say, "Well, how does this differ from any prayer I might say to ask God to help those people now?" It differs because, specifically, it is the form of benevolent magic that you can say for others, and the level of cooperation will be exactly the same, and the outcome will be benevolent—just like with benevolent magic, but it works for others.

Granted, the words might sound very simple, very simplistic, but you will find that you yourself will feel better. You won't take on the pain and suffering from others. You won't be frustrated from not being able to do anything in the moment about the situation. And it might very well be supporting that aid, comfort and love come to that person from all those beings—man, woman, child, boy, girl, dog, animal, who knows—who can help him or her.

Now, there are many advantages to saying this. Think about it: How many times have you had a friend, a relative, a loved one, even an acquaintance or maybe someone you've heard about whom you feel good about, maybe that person is in the hospital not feeling good. You've said your prayers for her—this is not meant to eliminate your prayers—but you also say your living prayer for her. You say—and I will pick a name at random—"I am asking that Millie's experience in the hospital be completely benevolent for her, and that her operation," say the name of that, "be successful, and that she be able to return home," for instance, or "return to work," (whatever fits in) "as quickly and as comfortably as possible."

If you feel a little warmth or a little energy that feels good, then just sit there for a moment and let that be there. And after a while, maybe in the case of saying it at bedtime, you might fall asleep. That's okay. In the case of saying it under your breath or at work, the energy will come and then it will go.

The energy has a lot to do with bringing about the benevolent results. The energy is literally the Creator (I'm making a triangle here with the fingers and the thumbs) . . . the energy is the feeling of the Creator interacting with your soul and the souls of all beings—three things—to bring this about in the most speedy, loving and benevolent way as much as possible. So, you see, this is a system that will look for potential assistance you can give this way for others.

Ask for What You Want

You must ask for what you want, not for what you don't want. Your body is involved in creation with Creator and all beings. Your body does not uncreate things. Your body might change the form of things, and physics will tell you that mass cannot be obliterated, it just changes form. So your body is constantly involved, working with Creator and angels and all kinds of beings like that and other people, of course, to create.

So sometimes when you ask—and many of you have said this—"Oh, I just don't want to experience that anymore. Just please, never again," your body doesn't hear that as uncreation. Your body will probably hear that as, "That experience was not good for me, and I don't want to experience it that way ever again." But your body will also hear that as, "The experience is desired, but in a different way."

See, if you know this, then this is a big clue for you to know how creation works on Earth and, to a degree, in other places. Please don't ask for what you don't want. Always ask for what you do want, because your body knows exactly how to do its part, as do the bodies of all other souls know how to do their part (consciously or unconsciously) to bring about and to create.

Resolution Is a Form of Creation

You are called in these many books by this channel members of the Explorer Race, and the Explorer Race is not a group of light-skinned people or dark-skinned people. The Explorer Race is all human beings on Earth. As members of the Explorer Race, you are here to learn many things. One of the things you are here to learn is to be able to create benevolently and also how to resolve things, even things that were not of your making, so that resolution will be possible.

Someday you will go out to the stars—as you see now, ships are going out, space stations, space capsules, men on the Moon, all that. Someday you'll go out and meet people from other planets. Many times they will share things with you that you will be thrilled to know. Other times you will share things with them because you on Earth will be experts on how to resolve things that other people don't know how to resolve.

Granted, those beings might have tremendously advanced technology. They might have very integrated and benevolent spirituality. But sometimes they will have conundrums, things they just can't fix as a society. You will be able to offer suggestions—sometimes they will seem to be very obvious to you. But the societies, although they cannot use your actual suggestions, will be inspired from your desire to create resolution, to fix something, and they will be able to get ideas and inspirations on their own.

This is one of the great gifts you will offer when you travel out into space. It is because of this that your bodies are set up by Creator to always be involved in creation. Resolution is a form of creation, and you all have to resolve things almost all the time. When you are a child, you have to figure out how shoelaces work—not an easy task for a youngster. As you grow up and get older, you have to figure out how the car goes this way and that way when you drive, or how you work the computer, or how you fix up something that somebody else seems to have left only partly done. In short, you're constantly involved with resolution.

Resolution is a form of creation. Your physical body is set up to do that; it's not set up to *not* do something. So if you know how the system works, you can work in the system a lot better. Always ask for what you want, not for what you don't want.

It's Important to Say What You Mean

This is also important in living prayer, when you are asking for things for other people. Remember, it will feel stilted sometimes. You might be stuck for words. If you find that you've said benevolent magic or living prayer and you've stumbled over the words—and this will often happen, even for experts at this—stop, wait a few minutes and start over and say it again. It's important to say it the way you want to say it all the way through without stumbling over the words any more than you can help.

For some of you, you might occasionally stumble over words more than others. Just say it as best you can. But for everybody else, if you don't usually stumble over words that much, then go back, just stop. If you stop right in the middle of the living prayer, wait a few minutes and then say it over again; it'll be just fine. If you go to the end and you realize you've stumbled over words and said something you didn't want to say or maybe it wasn't the best way to say it, then wait a few minutes and say it over again the way you want to say it.

The reason I am being very specific here is that you might find that you accidentally say something because of a lifetime of conditioning that you've had just being a human being in your culture and in your family. You might accidentally say a living prayer where you say something that you don't want, meaning, "Don't let that building collapse on those people in that earthquake." Uh-oh, wait a minute. You need to say it differently. Using that example, you might say, "I am asking that the people inside that building that has suffered damage be safe until they can be rescued, and that the building be strong and

---

Living Prayer

"I am asking that the people inside that building that has suffered damage be safe until they can be rescued, and that the building be strong and stay strong and stable until everyone who can be rescued is out and everybody is safe in the most benevolent way it can be."

---

stay strong and stable until everyone who can be rescued is out and everybody is safe in the most benevolent way it can be."

See, that's what you're asking for, something that can be. You have to change it. You don't say, "Don't let the building fall down," because your bodies won't know how to do that, nor will the bodies of others in this cooperative system. But you can say, "that the building be strong, stable and firm until everyone's been rescued."

You can often say, "Protect me from something." How many times have you had to go someplace or do something where you might wish to feel protected, feel secure, feel safer than you normally do? In this case, you might say the benevolent-magic version of that, where you might say, "I request that my trip to

Benevolent Magic

"I request that my trip to this job interview be completely safe for me to get there, that I feel safe and am safe while I'm there, and that my return also be that way in the most benevolent way for me, and that this result in the most benevolent outcome for me."

this job interview," then say the name of the company and so on, "be completely safe for me to get there, that I feel safe and am safe while I'm there, and that my return also be that way in the most benevolent way for me, and that this result in the most benevolent outcome for me," like that.

So in the case of a living prayer to be safe, you might say, "I am asking that my trip to this place, for this job interview, be completely safe, and that I be protected and enjoy the trip as well, and that the interview go well, and that my return trip also be completely safe for me," period. You can ask for a roundtrip like that. I generally recommend, however, that you say living prayer or benevolent magic one way, and then on the way back, you say it again, but you don't have to.

Living Prayer

"I am asking that my trip to this place, for this
job interview, be completely safe, and that I be
protected and enjoy the trip as well, and that the
interview go well, and that my return trip
also be completely safe for me."

Living Prayer for Yourself and Others

You don't just say living prayers for others; sometimes you can say them for yourself. You do say them for others as in my examples, but you can also say living prayers for yourself. And sometimes you can say a living prayer for yourself *and* others, see? But you always and only say benevolent magic for yourself, even though sometimes it might include others. I've told you how to do that.

Now, I want to give you an example where you might say a living prayer that involves yourself and others. Say you're in the earthquake zone and things are not quite right. Then you might say, "I am asking that I be completely safe as I move from this earthquake zone to some safer place, and that others around me are also safe and will be rescued benevolently for them as well." Say something like that, so it's more flexible, you see?

Living Prayer
"I am asking that I be completely safe as I move from this earthquake zone to some safer place, and that others around me are also safe and will be rescued benevolently for them as well."

Say there is a big storm coming, the weatherman on TV is predicting it. Then you might reasonably ask, "I am asking that I be completely safe in this storm, and that my family and community be safe as well."

Living Prayer

"I am asking that I be completely safe in this storm, and that my family and community be safe as well."

Benevolent Magic Must Be Benevolent for Everyone

Benevolent magic will not work unless it is benevolent for everyone. I want to be crystal clear with what I mean by that. Say you are asking for benevolent magic for some purpose for yourself that might even be good for others for all you know, or maybe you do know that it would be. In this case—as it is with living prayer, I might add—it is not possible for it to work at all unless everyone experiences benevolence. This means that whatever little thing they might have to do to cooperate—little things, big things—everything feels fine to everyone.

In some cases, people might do a big thing, but it doesn't make any difference to them. They could do it this way or that way. Instead of doing it that way, they end up doing it this way, and it's perfectly fine—it works for them. Maybe it'll be a big thing for you, maybe not. In any event, that's how it works.

It cannot work any other way unless it feels fine to everyone. To all souls, all beings, it has to feel fine. If it doesn't feel fine, it simply won't work. That's all. But there's not resentment that lasts forever.

Devas, deities, beings do not resent and distrust human beings. If anything, they decide that human beings (or those human beings in that place who are trying to do these things or cause them to do something) are just not ready to act benevolently for themselves and others at this time, and they step back. Those beings take a big step back, and they wait and let you work things out on your own—sometimes not very nicely. So they just do not cooperate with anything other than benevolence.

Benevolent Magic Can Be Very Freeing

This can literally liberate people all over the world by saying these words and then going on with their lives. You do not say benevolent magic or living prayer instead of doing things. You say benevolent magic and living prayer, and then you go ahead, continuing to strive toward what you are doing.

If you're asking for a parking space in front of your beauty parlor, you don't say benevolent magic and living prayer, and then just stop and sit there in the middle of the street. You continue to drive up the street until you find, perhaps, a good parking space. It may not be right in front of the beauty parlor, but it'll be as close as possible. Perhaps someone will drive out just as you're pulling up and you'll get a space that's better than you might have expected, so that's good.

I'm not guaranteeing that. It's a request. It will or maybe won't happen, but it will happen in the best possible way. The most benevolent way will occur. Most of the time, in some way, it'll be influencing things. If it doesn't happen, there might be another reason.

Maybe, in this example, because you had to go an extra block for a parking space, you actually wind up parking in front of some place, and when you get out of your car, you see an old friend. Or perhaps you happen to walk by a shop when you're on your way back to the beauty parlor and you say, "Wow! There's something I always needed"—something like that. You have to realize that the most benevolent outcome may not always be whatever thought you have that seems to be the best thing.

Benevolent magic can be very freeing for people, and it can be used by people even in desperate situations. Say you are a soldier in a war. If you're thinking, "My unit's going out today; I'm really, really worried," you can say, "I request that our mission today be completely safe, that we are able to accomplish our mission in the most benevolent way, and that this have the most benevolent outcome." You don't say "for me." In that case, it involves your unit and other people. Just say, "the most benevolent outcome," period.

<hr>

Benevolent Magic

"I request that our mission today be completely safe, that we are able to accomplish our mission in the most benevolent way, and that this have the most benevolent outcome."

<hr>

Now I will tell you how that could turn out. This could change the mission. Perhaps they say, "Take this stuff, go down the road and take it to those people who need it." So you drive down the road and you bring supplies. Normally you meet people on the way who are shooting at you, and normally you shoot back and people get killed, hurt, maimed, whatever.

In this case, you might even have people in your unit who because they've been in the war a long time and they've had their friends and their buddies wounded and maybe been wounded themselves, they're just waiting to shoot somebody who's going to shoot at them. Well, it could just be that nobody shoots at you and you don't shoot back at anybody else. You get there completely benevolently; nobody got hurt on either side. That's the most benevolent outcome, because the most benevolent outcome has to be benevolent for everybody.

Now, I'm not guaranteeing that this is going to change the world overnight. It is a request you make, but you still have to get in your truck and go on down the road and take this stuff from point A to point B. So you have to take action, but you still say this request. And maybe, just maybe, things are more benevolent than they would have been.

Say you're at home and you're worried about your loved one who's in a war somewhere, fighting far away or even fighting not that far away. Then you say, "I am asking that my loved one," say the name or say the unit, whatever, "be completely safe in," and then you say the place where that person is, generally the country, for instance, or at least the continent, "and come home to me," for instance—or you might even say, "and come home," period. Maybe your loved one is not coming home to you; maybe he or she doesn't live with you. Maybe this is a loved one like your father, and you're already married, living with somebody else.

Living Prayer

"I am asking that my loved one be completely safe in _____ and come home."

Don't Ask Over and Over Again

So you can say a living prayer anytime you want. Generally, if you say a living prayer about a subject, I recommend that you wait at least a day before you say it about that same subject again. And try to use different words, if you can, that accomplish the same purpose. However, if you've stumbled over words and you don't think you've said it just right, you can say it again after you wait a few minutes. But if you're saying benevolent magic about something specific (maybe you need a new car or maybe you need a new job), just say that once unless you're going to change the words, the meaning, and the desire is different. Then say it again, but change the words.

Benevolent magic is not like a prayer, something you say over and over and over again for comforting reasons or for religious discipline, for instance. It is something you say once. Living prayer, however, can be said for you or for others many times.

So if you have a loved one in the war, you can say it more than once. Try to change the form of what you say or what you ask. Don't ask it over and over and over again because your creator self, your soul, your portion of Creator working with Creator and all beings, they got it when you said it once. Your body, your soul and all parts of you (including your connection to Creator) will be working on it immediately after you say it.

But if something else comes up—maybe you're talking about a specific battle your loved one is in, in the case of the soldier, and then she is some place else. Maybe she's even going on leave, but she can't come home. Then you might say a living prayer for her that she is completely safe and will have fun on her leave—something like that.

After all, stories abound—you've heard about them—stories that kind of make you chuckle: "Oh, I went through the war completely. Four years," you hear from soldiers, or "two years" or "one year." "I went through the whole war, came home, tripped over a bicycle and broke my foot." Of course, after your foot heals, this becomes a family joke. You all laugh about that.

So you might say something like that, if your loved one is coming home, has been through that: "I'm asking that my loved one on his trip home here be completely safe and have a benevolent experience to get here," like that. You can see that this applies to lots of different situations. But if you ever try and say something in some way that would hurt others, it just won't work.

Living Prayer

"I'm asking that my loved one on his trip home here be completely safe and have a benevolent experience to get here."

Magic Is the Natural Element of Life

Why don't I call it benevolent prayer? Because prayers are long established with religions and even philosophies. We need to call it magic because magic is the natural element of life. When you are a child and you see your first flower, and you see it closed up at night and then mom or dad or one of your brothers or sisters says, "Look!" and it's opened up in the day, that's magical to you. You know when you are a little one that magic is natural and normal, and it's intended to be natural and normal in beauty, such as flowers opening up.

Or such as yourself, as a child, when you feel like you want to get older: "Oh, if I can *just* get older, if I can *just* get to the fifth grade!" Then eventually you say, "If I can *just* to high school," then, "If I can *just* get to work or get to college." Things do change—sometimes, apparently, magically. You know if you say, "If I can just have that first date. If I can just get that first dance," then sometimes out of the blue, there it is, and there's no logical explanation for it.

Magic is normal and healthy. We need to define it as benevolent magic so you understand how the benevolent magic of Creator who created this universe and created Earth upon which you live, how that benevolent magic actually works by involving you as a kind of a Creator junior to support bringing about benevolent creations for yourself.

You have your junior Creator badge on, but you won't expect people to treat you as a religious object. You are who you are, a portion of Creator, loved all the time by Creator, no matter what. After your life, sometimes you are surprised and shocked at things you did, and you might regret them. Creator is still pouring love on you because Creator knows you're trying to do the best you can. You tell Creator, "I'll do better next time," and Creator says, "Okay, here's your chance."

There is a connotation now about magic that it's supernatural, but we are attempting to bring an understanding that it is absolutely natural. Supernatural seems to be something beyond your grasp—and it is when it comes to creating universes and planets like Creator does. But this is something that, even though very often it works magically . . . it doesn't always work *the way* you want, but it works magically to bring about *what* you want.

You know you've been a part of it, you've been involved in bringing it about, even though you don't exactly understand how it happened. So it's a way of involving you in Creator's natural benevolent magic that Creator uses to open up universes lovingly for Creator's children. And it also involves cooperation, which is a step toward unity.

This Is Not Meant to Replace Your Religion

Now, some religious people might ask, "Is it okay to say, 'Jesus, I am asking,' 'God, I am asking'?" Try it both ways. If you want to involve the name of your religious deity, try it.

In my experience, it may not work as well, because when you say the name of your deity . . . you know how your religion works. Your religion works, say, in the case of Christianity—and in particular, in Catholicism—with your prayers, where your prayers go through the priest to beyond, to your deity. And this way your priest's job is to make sure that they are as pure and clear as possible so that when they go to the deity, they arrive in the best possible way. I'm greatly simplifying this, but that's essentially it.

So if you say the name of the deity, your thoughts and feelings from a lifetime of training (or as long as you've been involved in that religion) will automatically click into limiting the scope of the benevolent magic to functioning within the stratum of the rules of that religion. This is not to say don't. Try it. If you want to say it that way, try it. I'm not saying don't. In my belief system, it will work better without invoking the name of your deity or beloved religious person.

You can do your religion in your regular prayer all the time. Just ask for what you want in your regular prayer and then do this as well on the side. It is something that is not meant to be instead of prayer. So try it both ways, that's what I'd say, and then see the result. I'd recommend doing it without saying the name of the deity, but I want you to feel free to experiment and try it that way if you choose.

If someone says that in his religious training, he is to say prayers for everybody else and he's not supposed to ask for anything for himself because he feels that that would be selfish . . . when people say that to you, say, "I completely understand and sympathize with that philosophy. I want things that are good to happen to everyone else too, and that's why sometimes I use living prayer for that." And you can go into that if you want to at that moment or later, because you can also say this: "You have to ask yourself, and I've asked myself," you might say, "that Creator created me lovingly. Therefore, I must be worth creating. If this is so, then I can ask for things for me."

Now, I know that some people would not feel comfortable with that. I'm not expecting that everyone will want to do this, but some people might wish to try, especially if they've got something pressing in their life or something urgent or just something that's been nagging at them for a long time or some other problem that they want to perhaps be able to get through.

So if you feel selfish or guilty for saying this . . . I grant that you may feel that. The selfish, guilty feeling, if it's overwhelming, may restrict somewhat the welcoming of what you're asking for. You have to ask yourself, "Am I willing or open to allowing this to come to me?" You may not know the answer to that.

I am saying that Creator created you completely open and lovingly brought about your creation. Granted, mom and dad fell in love and they came together and you popped out eventually, but Creator had something to do with it because Creator created mom and dad and all the moms and dads before you. So if Creator did that, it wasn't an accident.

You have to understand that benevolent magic and living prayer are going to be somewhat controversial, and they might stimulate thought, but one of my beliefs is that human beings are valuable, each and every one. Granted, some of them might seem to be more valuable than others at different times, and even parts of your life may seem to be more valuable than other parts at different times, but Creator created you lovingly and loves you, period. Therefore, I feel that asking for something for yourself is acceptable, especially when you have your other forms of prayer for your religion and living prayer to ask for things for others.

This is not meant to replace your religion, only to support and sustain your life in some other ways. Some people like to call it a tool, something you can use. If you have a heavy wrench, you might try to pound in a nail, but if you use a hammer, it might work better. But in this case, the tool is something that incorporates the creatorship in all beings that has been freely given to you by Creator because Creator loves you. You wouldn't be here if Creator didn't love you.

Sometimes the Most Benevolent Outcome Is Not What You'd Expect

Another question you might have concerns that example of you at home and your loved one overseas in battle. What if it is time for that soldier to die and that is the most benevolent outcome? Well, that will happen. You might be asking for his safety, but it might just be, in the case of some horrible war wound, that it is time for him to die, and you wouldn't want him to suffer and go on suffering. You'd want him to die as quickly and as painlessly as possible. Of course, you would never ask for that. You would ask for him to be safe and to come home to you.

Well, this is not magic in the sense of distorting or forcing. There is no forcing. It's always and only benevolent. If the most benevolent result would be that the person would quickly and as painlessly as possible die, then that would be a comfort of sort perhaps. Perhaps your son's or your daughter's or your cousin's or your nephew's commanding officer will write to you and say, "He was a wonderful soldier; he served very well. I noticed that this person got along well in his unit and was well-liked. And I remember him for this or that complimentary reason. This person was very brave and served the country very well. And just to let you know, the death was almost instantaneous. I don't think he felt a thing."

Many people have received letters like this from commanding officers who wanted to make a personal touch and let you know that, according to eyewitnesses, there wasn't a lot of suffering. I'm not saying that this is always the case. I'm just saying that many of you have seen letters like this or heard about them. The idea here is that whatever does occur, we accept that that *was* the most benevolent outcome.

That's the case, just like the other incidents or catastrophes or disasters that you hear about in the news all the time. When you think back on those situations, the best thing you would've hoped for is that the people died as quickly and as painlessly as possible, and that does happen sometimes in some disasters. It happens—it's all over so fast that they didn't suffer. They didn't even know it. They discovered they were dead after the fact when the angels came and embraced them and said, "It's time to move on." This happens. Other times, it's other ways.

But either way, when you die and your body returns to the Earth, you—your personality as you know yourself to be—go on. Your personality never dies. It goes on because when Creator creates a soul, Creator never uncreates that soul. So that soul goes on.

This is why you can walk down the street sometime and you meet someone that you've never met, and before you know it, in a few minutes you just seem to be as close of friends as many people you've known for years. Maybe at some other time, in some other place, in some other creation that Creator had, you were good friends there.

Life goes on. And the basic characteristics of your personality are perpetuated through the years, through the lifetimes and through incarnations. When Creator creates a soul, it goes on forever, regardless of what body you may be born in. Your body lives sixty, eighty years—maybe more, maybe less in some cases. You die and you go on in some other form somewhere.

Ask for the Unexpected

Now, there is another thing: Tom Moore has been very involved in the creation of the wording structures that can be used by anyone and has been strongly advocating benevolent magic in the form of which he refers to it as most benevolent outcomes [see Moore's article in the December 2002 issue of the *Sedona Journal of Emergence!*]. He did not on his own create this, but through his own practice as a spiritual man, he has done a lot to popularize it so far. He has found that there is another thing you can say sometimes. You don't say it all the time, but you might at times when you're saying benevolent magic, especially if you're going to do something, like you're going to go to a meeting.

Maybe you're going to go to a sales meeting, and you might say your benevolent magic for the most benevolent outcome for that. And then, almost as an afterthought, you might tag on, "And I would like also that I even have unexpected good things that come about, that come as a pleasant surprise that exceeds my expectations," and any other way you want to say that. I want you to be, to feel a little spontaneous saying that.

Benevolent Magic
"And I would like also that I even have unexpected good things that come about, that come as a pleasant surprise that exceeds my expectations."

I would recommend that in the future you say, "I'm open to the possibility that my desires, my expectations or my requests will be exceeded by the event."

This is a great gift. It implies a maturity in and a movement into an expansion of your natural self to even be given this type of information.

Benevolent Magic

"I'm open to the possibility that my desires, my expectations or my requests will be exceeded by the event."

Create Solutions by Asking for the Impossible

I think that it is important to say that the world has come to a place where you need more. You need to be able to create solutions to apparently unsolvable problems. Groups of people who have been battling for a long time are past the point of being able to forgive one another, so it seems. And yet you might ask for it in living prayer or benevolent magic, as well as in the other ways you ask and the other ways you strive to bring about resolution.

It's possible to go beyond what seems to be possible to bring about resolution. In short, don't limit benevolent-magic requests and your living prayer. Don't limit them to what appears to be possible. Feel perfectly free to ask for the impossible in your own thoughts, because the whole point of benevolent magic is that it will very often exceed anything you can actually think about as a resolution. It goes beyond thought, and that's the point of magic.

When that child, that baby, goes out and toddles around and sees flowers and cats and dogs and trees, and she has that look of wonder on her face—you've seen it, many of you—you know that that child knows in her thoughts and feelings that this is magic. You all deserve such magic, and you deserve to participate in the creation of benevolent magic. That's why, in this book, we are cooperating to bring that to you, to offer it to you, to encourage you to use it and to suggest that you enjoy your experience with it as much as possible.

2

How to Use Benevolent Magic and Living Prayer in Your Day-to-Day Life

Reveals the Mysteries
November 22, 2004

❦❦❦❦❦❦❦

We want to give the readers a jump-start, so to speak, so that they will get an idea of how this thing works. Once they have a dozen examples applied to different situations, then they can guess on the basis of those how their particular individual desires can be framed within the context of this material.

Adapting Benevolent Magic and Living Prayer to Different Situations

Since in saying the benevolent magic, the words are so specific and it requires, "Say this; don't say that" . . . we've gone over that a bit; that's pretty specific. But the living prayer is very simple. Then you might just say this: Say you're in danger. Then just immediately say, "I am asking for help in the most benevolent way for me now."

Living Prayer

"I am asking for help in the most benevolent way for me now."

But if you have a few moments, for those of you who are used to saying benevolent magic or have come to be used to it, you might be able to say, "I request that I receive all the immediate help I can receive in the most benevolent way for me, and that this have the most benevolent outcome for me to bring about my safety and my comfort"—like that. We can adapt it a bit, you see.

Benevolent Magic

"I request that I receive all the immediate help I can receive in the most benevolent way for me, and that this have the most benevolent outcome for me to bring about my safety and my comfort."

In the case of saying benevolent magic, this might be something that you know is a discomforting situation. For instance, let's say that you're driving on the freeway or the highway, and there is somebody who's weaving around on the road. You slow down, but the person doesn't seem to know what he's doing—perhaps he's inebriated or perhaps he is sick and he's not quite clear. In short, help has not arrived yet.

Of course, if somebody's in the car, you call for help because someone might be sick and so on. But until that arrives, you say either your benevolent magic or your living prayer, and once you've said it for yourself and waited for a few minutes, if the situation persists, you can then say a living prayer for the person in the car. You might say, "I am asking that this person or people in this car also receive all of the help they need right now from all those beings who can help them."

Living Prayer

"I am asking that this person or people in this car also receive all of the help they need right now from all those beings who can help them."

Then perhaps the police or perhaps a friend will come along and get that person to pull over, make sure he is all right, maybe call for an ambulance or so-and-so, or maybe find out that it's somebody's ten-year-old brother who thought he was big enough to drive the car or something like that. People sometimes see cars going down the road on their own, and they don't see the little head peeking out who thought perhaps that it was just fine to drive the car because he could drive the tractor just fine, but this was not the same thing. You hear about stories like that.

There are other circumstances you can imagine, sometimes much more dangerous. The benevolent magic in this book is intended to give you something to start with. There will be future books of this nature that are easy to carry around, that are portable. There will be other things we will talk about in the future that will also give you methods to be safe and give you other trainings. And someday we may even compile this into a larger book and add more material for those of you who wish to go into this in a deeper study fashion.

But for right now, we feel so strongly about this that we want to get this out to you as soon as possible, since we know that many of you are not feeling safe in your physical world right now, whatever place you're living in. You would like to feel safer; you would like to have good things happen. You'd like to create a safe, benevolent environment, not only for yourself and your family and your friends, but also for the world, so that everybody can learn how to get along together and enjoy the variety of different peoples without getting stuck on the discomfort about something new.

Ask to Remember to Do Benevolent Magic

For most of you, when you get up in the morning, one of your first stops is the bathroom. And very often, you may look in the mirror. Sometimes you smile; sometimes you frown. But I'd like you to have something on the mirror in very bright can't-miss-it letters. You don't have to write right on the mirror, but you can put a little sign there—like red crayon on light-colored paper. And I'd like it to say: "Remember, benevolent magic and living prayer are for you," period.

> "Remember, benevolent magic and living prayer are for you."

Some of you have children who might want to do this. Ask the kids to write it, because when you see your youngsters' writing, it's going to make you smile—you know it is. Because anything they write or draw always makes you smile lovingly when you look at it. But if you want to do it on your own, go ahead.

Now, you might reasonably ask, "Why are you saying to do it in crayon?" It doesn't have to be in crayon, but the reason I recommend crayon is that it's likely to draw your attention because most of you do not use crayons anymore. For those of you who have children, crayons will be around. (And for those of you who don't, you can easily get crayons.) It's kind of fun.

This will be childlike, and it's much more likely to draw your attention if it's something that is out of the ordinary in the way of signs that you might post for yourself. You know, you might put up, "Remember Charlie's birthday," or you might put up, "Don't forget about that _____," whatever important thing. You'll write that, but some sign in red crayon is probably not the sort of thing that you normally make.

Ask for Anything—No Limitations

Now, I would like to say that the reason this book exists is to let you know that benevolent magic exists and to give you some suggestions to start with. When you start using it, you may not say it very much because you can't imagine what might be possible to say.

So we're going to give you some suggestions for various situations that might come up in your life to give you—how can we say?—kind of like some trial runs. And after a while, you'll be able to say it for the simplest things and even the more complex things, such as an unhealthy situation.

Ask for Personal Safety

But you don't say "an unhealthy situation" because that would be very vague and would be not understood clearly by all beings. Rather, you would say, for instance . . . we'll bring up something dramatic: In a situation where, say, a woman is being mistreated by her husband for whatever reason—maybe he drinks; who knows?—she might say, "I request that my personal safety be guaranteed for me now in the most benevolent way for me now, and that this have the most benevolent outcome for me."

> "I request that my personal safety be guaranteed for
> me now in the most benevolent way for me now, and
> that this have the most benevolent outcome for me."

Suppose she has children in the same situation.
Then she might say, "I request that the personal safety
for me and my children," say their names (first names
are sufficient), "be completely guaranteed in the most
benevolent way for me." You're saying something for
somebody else, but as a mother, if these are children
you're overseeing . . . and I'm talking about little kids,
okay? "Little kids," by definition, means under fif-
teen, because if they are sixteen, seventeen, eighteen,
they can probably take care of themselves. If you
want to, though, you can include "the eighteen-year-
old and down." Then say the rest of the words as they
were said.

> "I request that the personal safety for me and
> my children be completely guaranteed in
> the most benevolent way for me."

If you do that, I would recommend that you do a follow-up. Wait a few minutes, and do a follow-up living prayer. If you wait longer than a few minutes, that's all right—do a follow-up, since you are saying something for somebody else. And you can say, "I am asking that the personal safety of myself and my children," Dottie, Mary, Joe, whatever their names are, "be guaranteed immediately and indefinitely now in a way that is benevolent for us all," period—something like that. You can see that I'll sometimes add variations, and the reason I'm doing this is that I want you to consider adapting this to your own system while staying within the format.

> ### Living Prayer
> "I am asking that the personal safety of myself and my children be guaranteed immediately and indefinitely now in a way that is benevolent for us all."

Ask for Money and Abundance

Just say, "I am asking that my personal income increase in an increasing way and in the most benevolent way for me now, and that this result in the most benevolent outcome." Then pause for a little while, perhaps for thirty seconds. Then say, "for me."

Living Prayer

"I am asking that my personal income increase in an increasing way and in the most benevolent way for me now, and that this result in the most benevolent outcome [pause for thirty seconds] for me."

The reason we pause in that case is that your personal income is probably going to be distributed to various people, and we want that to have the most benevolent outcome for all beings. So you pause to allow that to get settled energetically for all beings, and then you make it clear by saying "for me" because *you're* asking. It's about *your* personal income—you want more personal income for yourself. But the pause allows that energy to spread around and that request to spread around because other people will very often be benevolently served by your personal income as you distribute it.

Now, if you want to say it in the form of a living prayer, you might say it. You can say those anytime you want, according to my suggestions—perhaps once a day about the subject. If you say it more often, then try to say it differently every time, not just changing one word, but changing the meaning.

It's most important when you say benevolent magic and living prayer to have feeling about it, to want it, to need it—meaning that it's okay to have feeling. It's not something you say, like words. This is not "Parking between four and six P.M. acceptable." It's not words you just say. It's good to have feeling, the want, the desire, the need. If they're there, try to welcome your feelings, and then say the benevolent magic or living prayer.

So you might say, in this case of increased income, "I am asking that my income continue to increase and that it become predictable and reliable so I'll know that I'm going to get what I need and more to cover all my expenses so that I can feel safe, comfortable and

Living Prayer

"I am asking that my income continue to increase and that it become predictable and reliable so I'll know that I'm going to get what I need and more to cover all my expenses so that I can feel safe, comfortable and happy."

happy"—something like that. You're saying what you want to feel. You want to feel safe. You want to feel comfortable. And of course, you want to feel happy.

Don't let people tell you—as it happens and people talk—that there's only so much to go around when it comes to wealth and money. There's nothing wrong with being wealthy. You can all do it. It's all acceptable. I assure you, Creator would not have allowed wealthiness if Creator did not feel that wealthiness wasn't good. It's not something bad. So feel free to ask.

For instance, you might say, "I am asking for my personal income and my personal resources to increase and develop in such a way as I feel wealthy, and that this occur benevolently for me so that I may be happy and comfortable." Say something like that. But don't say "that I may be happy and comfortable" to justify it. Rather, you indicate that those feelings would be ones

Living Prayer

"I am asking for my personal income and my personal resources to increase and develop in such a way as I feel wealthy, and that this occur benevolently for me so that I may be happy and comfortable."

you might feel. And if you feel, say, warmth—and we discussed warmth before in these pages of these various books—or if you happen to feel comfortable or feel happy after saying that, just let that feeling be there. Don't suppress it. That's part of the creation process.

Creator wants you to be comfortable and happy. Just know that that's possible. Don't let anybody tell you it isn't possible for you. If someone tells you that, then you say, "Well, that's fine if you want to believe that. I believe otherwise." If you don't feel comfortable saying that, you don't have to. Just know that you can believe otherwise.

Ask to Find the Right Work

Say, "I request that I have wonderful work to do that allows me to feel happy and fulfilled as much as possi-

---

Benevolent Magic

"I request that I have wonderful work to do that allows me to feel happy and fulfilled as much as possible and provides benevolent and nurturing income for me as well, and that this occur in the most benevolent way for me, and that this have the most benevolent outcome for me."

---

ble and provides benevolent and nurturing income for me as well, and that this occur in the most benevolent way for me, and that this have the most benevolent outcome for me."

Ask for Healthy Relationships

Say, "I am asking that I experience the most wonderful mate for me, that she or he like and love me just the way I am, and that I like and love him or her just the way he or she is in the most benevolent way for me, and that this result in the most benevolent outcome for me." You can, if you like, at the end of that, pause for thirty seconds or so. Then say, "for me," because you are asking for someone to come in.

> *Living Prayer*
>
> *"I am asking that I experience the most wonderful mate for me, that she or he like and love me just the way I am, and that I like and love him or her just the way he or she is in the most benevolent way for me, and that this result in the most benevolent outcome [pause for thirty seconds] for me."*

Now, suppose this is a relationship associated with business, for instance. Then you might say, "I am asking that the perfect business partner or partners come to me now and make themselves known to me now in the most benevolent way for me, and that this result in the most benevolent outcome." Pause for about thirty seconds, maybe a little more, maybe a little less, and then say, "for me."

Now, there are other kinds of relationships. Let's bring up a few of those so you can see that this is a broad brush we're stroking with. Say, "I request that my relationship with my son," or daughter, sister, brother, husband, whoever you want to say, the name of someone you know, "that my relationship with," fill in the blank, "improve now and continue to improve in the most benevolent way for me, and that this have the

> "I request that my relationship with _____ improve
> now and continue to improve in the most benevolent
> way for me, and that this have the most benevolent
> outcome [pause for thirty seconds] for me."

most benevolent outcome," pause, "for me."

Does any other kind of relationship come to mind?
I've got another one: "I request that my relationship
with my beloved dog," cat, horse, whatever you have,
maybe a pet or even animals on your farm, "improve
steadily in the most benevolent way for me, and that
this result in the most benevolent outcome," then
pause for about a minute or two. Pause for a while,
because this is interspecies and we want this to have
plenty of time. If you want to pause a little longer,
that's fine, but no longer than three minutes if you
can help it. Then say, "for me."

> "I request that my relationship with my beloved pet
> improve steadily in the most benevolent way for
> me, and that this result in the most benevolent
> outcome [pause for two to three minutes] for me."

Ask for a Perfect Home

Let's do benevolent magic: "I request that the perfect home in the best place for me be revealed to me now and be easily attained by me now in the most benevolent way for me, and that this have the most benevolent outcome for me."

Benevolent Magic

"I request that the perfect home in the best place for me be revealed to me now and be easily attained by me now in the most benevolent way for me, and that this have the most benevolent outcome for me."

Now, some of you might have a husband, a wife, a partner, friends, family, whoever, who share the home with you, meaning that they live there regularly. In that case, you might say a living prayer: "I am asking that the best home that is available for me and my family," friends, whomever you live with (you can say their names if you like; just their first names are sufficient), "be made available right now for me," or you can say "us," if you like, "and that we know about it and can easily acquire access for as long as we need to that home in the most benevolent and comforting way for me"—or "us"—"now."

I would like to suggest, however, that if you're not absolutely certain that these other individuals are going to live with you in that home, as you might be, say, if they're your children or an uncle or aunt whom you're looking after, perhaps a grandma or grandpa, someone like that whom you're absolutely sure is going to live there . . . only say that. Only say the names of those whom you're absolutely certain are going to live with you—not people you want to live with you but you're not certain. It doesn't mean that it won't be supported that you get the home, but if you say the name of someone who, even if you don't know it, would just as soon not live with you, the living prayer probably won't work.

So the safest thing is to say it for you specifically, because you know you want it. You can't be certain if the other people want it in the circumstances that you are requesting. So that's a piece of advice, and it applies broadly to lots of other living prayers when you are asking for something for yourself and others.

Ask for Help for Beings Who Need Help

That's why the general living prayer, where you are asking something to support and nurture others, is so valuable. Because many times you won't have the facts and it isn't even something for you. For instance, you might say, "I am asking that all those people"—you could say "beings," if you like—"who need help in New Zealand receive all the help they need right now from all those beings"—"and people," you can say, or you can say "people"—"who can help them."

Living Prayer

"I am asking that all those beings who need help in _____ receive all the help they need right now from all those beings who can help them."

Now, I'm picking New Zealand as an example. Certainly you can think of other countries—China, Russia, Finland, Chile, Greece, Turkey, Israel, Syria, Lebanon—all kinds of other worthy and wonderful countries where perhaps you are concerned about the people, even if you don't know them or have never met them. It's a wonderful thing, and in order to make it crystal clear, the simplest way to say it is, "I am asking that all those beings in," such and such a place, "receive all the help they need from all those beings who can help them."

> #### Living Prayer
> "I am asking that all those beings in _____
> receive all the help they need from all those
> beings who can help them."

To make it even simpler for those of you who would like to say something . . . sometimes you watch the news and the net result of that is that you feel uncomfortable. You can't remember the names of places or things that happened because so much information went by so quickly. So then you simply say, "I am asking that all those beings who need help receive all the help from all those beings who can help them."

After all, you are a being. You are a human being, and there are other beings. All forms of existence are beings. Science will tell you that everything has motion, and from science's point of view, you might reasonably extrapolate that everything is alive. From my point of view, I know that everything is alive. And benevolent magic and living prayer are unifiers to support all beings and all life.

Ask for Health to Improve

In the case of health, we'll give variations on that. You might just say in general, "I request that my health improve, and that it become more easy for me to live in my body now in the most benevolent way for me, and that this have the most benevolent outcome for me."

> *"I request that my health improve, and that it become more easy for me to live in my body now in the most benevolent way for me, and that this have the most benevolent outcome for me."*

You might have a condition—perhaps long-term, perhaps short-term. I will pick something like that at random, or perhaps I will just allow you to fill in your condition as diagnosed from a physician, or perhaps you don't know the condition. Maybe you have your doctor's appointment next week, and your doctor has some knowledge about it—you've spoken to your doctor, and your doctor has said, "Well, you can take this for now and then come and see me in a couple of days," and so on.

Always call your doctor or your practitioner who helps you so you have some idea; it's especially helpful when you're saying your request here. So you might say, "I request that," and then you refer to your condition, "improve and become more gentle in my body so my health can become more benevolent for me, and that this result in the most benevolent outcome for me."

You might also say that as a living prayer: "I am
asking that my," fill in the blank, "improve now in the
gentlest, most comforting and speediest way for me
now." That's an example. We'll give other examples
from time to time. Those of you who have a computer, go to the website [www.lighttechnology.com]
and we'll add them when possible. We don't always
add things right away, but we'll add them when we
can. You can use this book on your own and maybe
support and discuss it with others so you can see how
else you might say these things.

Now, suppose you want to improve the health of
other beings. Perhaps you've heard about a disease

somewhere, perhaps it's mysterious, in another country that seems to be developing. Maybe a world organization such as the World Health Organization or others are concerned, or your own government's health organization is concerned, or your own community or your doctor or your broadcaster on your news program or your newspaper suggest concern. Then you can say, in the form of a living prayer, "I am asking that all those beings in," blank (you fill out the name of the country), "who are experiencing," and then if there's a name for it (the news or some other organization might have a name for it), "receive all the help they need right now from all those beings who can help them."

Living Prayer

"I am asking that all those beings in _____ who are experiencing _____ receive all the help they need right now from all those beings who can help them."

There's a follow-up to that, because this may not occur to you right off. And that is that you speak to the disease organism itself, even if it's not known, and you say, "I am asking that the form of life that is generating this disease and discomfort in," and you can say the place if you want to, or you can simply say, "in the people who are experiencing this, that this form of life mutate now into a benign form that will be gentle on all beings like those whom it's affecting now," or if you want to, you can say, "on all human beings." But you can see how this can easily be applied to diseases that might affect animals, for instance.

Living Prayer

"*I am asking that the form of life that is generating this disease and discomfort in the people who are experiencing this, that this form of life mutate now into a benign form that will be gentle on all beings like those whom it's affecting now.*"

If you have a ranch or a farm, this is important. You can say the same thing for your plants, but you can address the organism or organisms themselves because you'd be surprised. They might be perfectly comfortable—"they," speaking of them as a form of life—mutating (and they can do that) into some form where they're still alive but they do not cause discomfort or disease or harm of any sort to human beings, to plants, to animals, whomever you are asking it for. You'd be surprised how effective that can be at times.

Ask for Inspiration

You might say, "I request that my capacity to be inspired and my ability to interpret inspiration for the creation of my story occur now in the most benevolent way for me, and that this result in the most benevolent outcome for me." You say "for me" right away. You don't pause, even though it might be a story about other people. It might be something you're making up, such as a novel, or it might be something that you're researching as a newspaper reporter or a television news writer or a magazine person who writes. The reason you say "for me" immediately is that you are asking for your own process to work—*your* inspiration.

Benevolent Magic
"I request that my capacity to be inspired and my ability to interpret inspiration for the creation of my story occur now in the most benevolent way for me, and that this result in the most benevolent outcome for me."

Now, as a writer about news, since I'm using that as an example, you might say, "I request that I receive now all the cooperation I need to write a true, interesting story about," and then you can fill in the subject, "and that this story be presented," and then you can list your publication or TV station, for instance, "in the most benevolent way for me," (meaning, in this case—I'm interpreting as I go along—that your editor says, "Great story, let's run it"), "and that this result in the most benevolent outcome for me." This might mean, for instance, that your editor pats you on the back and maybe gives you that appraising eye that says, "There's hope for your career in the future," like that.

Benevolent Magic

"I request that I receive now all the cooperation I need to write a true, interesting story about _____, and that this story be presented in the most benevolent way for me, and that this result in the most benevolent outcome for me."

As a living prayer, in that case, you might ask, "I am asking that all those beings who can cooperate with me that I might write the best story do so now in the most benevolent way," pause in this case for about twenty or thirty seconds, "for me, and that this result in a fine story that I can present comfortably to others." Say something like that, because you're asking . . . you're going to pause and work benevolence in on that because many times, as anybody who writes stories for any reason knows, very often the cooperation of others is needed or required—even for people who write novels. It's often required, certainly for people who write topical stories.

Living Prayer

"I am asking that all those beings who can cooperate with me that I might write the best story do so now in the most benevolent way [pause for thirty seconds] for me, and that this result in a fine story that I can present comfortably to others."

Ask for Benevolent Political Decisions and Actions

You might say, for instance, "I am asking that my country's leaders be inspired benevolently and carry out benevolent policies for all those whom they affect, and that those policies serve the needs of all beings as much as possible." Do you see? It's not so difficult.

> "I am asking that my country's leaders be inspired
> benevolently and carry out benevolent policies for
> all those whom they affect, and that those policies
> serve the needs of all beings as much as possible."

But you see, when you say "benevolent," what it is, is that sometimes you want something and many times it's worthy—you want it, you want it to be good, you want things to be better for people. But very often in the case of governments, the people they serve do not have as many facts as the government has. Many times the government does not release all their facts because they are trying to protect other people, to keep them safe, but they know that these facts are true and sometimes they will act in ways that you don't understand.

I'm not trying to say that all government leaders are perfectly fine and good, and that you should just trust them. I am saying that this living prayer supports them to do the best they can in the most benevolent way for all beings, and it takes into account these extenuating circumstances that I used for an example just a moment ago.

If you have a specific issue, a proposition you would like the government to pass or perhaps a law you'd like them to pass—perhaps something that you would like to change in the global situation that your government may be involved in or that you would prefer that your government be involved in and it isn't at the moment—you can ask, "I am asking . . ." Always begin a living prayer like this because this covers broad communities.

Say, "I am asking that," and you can say the name of your president or premier or secretary or something like that (whatever's the proper terminology for your form of government). You can say, "our leader," whatever you wish to say, but say it in a benevolent way, with no putdowns. If you say it in a putdown way or in a wisecracking way, I guarantee you that it will not work because benevolent magic and living prayer work because it's benevolent for everybody. Therefore, all souls are happy to cooperate.

So say, "I am asking that," and fill in the name of your government leaders or just say the leaders of blank government (maybe it's not even your government; it might be another country), "be inspired to carry out the most benevolent policies that will serve the needs of the people of our whole country"—or in some cases, "the world,"—"and that this result in a happier, more nurtured and comforted global community," in the case of some major event. It is important that the living prayer take into account that all souls are being asked to cooperate. All beings are being asked to cooperate, so it has to be benevolent for all beings.

Living Prayer

"I am asking that our leader be inspired to carry out the most benevolent policies that will serve the needs of the people of our whole country, and that this result in a happier, more nurtured and comforted global community."

When the government makes decisions, let it take into account the needs of the Earth and the people as well as the needs of business and government. Say, "I am asking that the people in my government," and say what government, maybe the United States, "serve the planet in the most benevolent way that they can." Keep it simple and direct. That's what you're actually asking for; that's what you want.

Sometimes you'll find that your living prayers will go on and have too many words because you're trying to be specific—because in your society, as you know, the tendency in order to create a very clear, specific point is to add more words. But sometimes it's better to use less and to make those words very clear.

They might sound highly simplistic. In this case, you might say, for instance . . . pick a public park, let's say the Grand Canyon. Say, "I am asking that my government leaders do all they can to support and nurture all the beings who live in or visit the Grand Canyon in the most benevolent way that they can."

You could say that for anything. You could say the Gobi Desert. You could say anything. And it can be applied that way, you see? It needs to always be said in a way . . . you don't have to say "my great and glorious leaders," you don't have to say something complimentary. You just have to allow them . . . you have to literally allow them to *be* without qualifying or describing and without prompting some discomfort in them.

Ask for Mother Earth to Replenish Herself

This is an aside, but I'll give you an example so you can see where I'm going with this. If you take uranium out of the Earth and then you turn it into other things and then you have radioactive waste, the best place to put it back is where you found the uranium in the first place, especially if that mine is no longer in operation, because that land will be in a position to reabsorb anything radioactive. Of course, you're going to encase it and so on, but it's going to radiate just a little bit even through that encasement. It won't radiate a lot, but a little bit, and that radiation will be better off there in the best way you can establish that.

Given that point of view that I have stated and that others have stated through Robert, I would say something like this: "I am asking that Mother Earth replenish herself and experience benevolent support from all beings to replenish all portions of herself, in the most benevolent way, that humans on Earth have removed or changed."

Now, in this case we say "the most benevolent way" and we don't say "for Mother Earth," because of course, Mother Earth's benevolent ways for herself might be volcanoes or tidal waves. So we just want it to be the most benevolent way broadly. Even though Mother Earth knows what to do, knows how to do it, in this way you are saying something that genuinely refers to something you'd like to happen.

Notice that even though I mentioned the atomic waste, I'm saying in this case that we want Mother Earth to replenish herself. And we want support from all beings for this to happen. So we're essentially asking all souls to cooperate in the benevolent magic that it will take for these things to magically reappear in Mother Earth's body in all the places she needs them.

Oil in Mother Earth's body is . . . she uses it to lubricate her body and all of these things. Even gas domes are like pressure areas that hold various parts of her body.

I understand that your society is set up in such a way that you've discovered uses for these things and that you know how to convert them so your society is more supported, but we need Mother Earth to be replenished. In this case, we are asking all beings, including all your souls and all beings, to support Mother Earth to re-create these things for herself, given that for some time now you will continue to remove some of these things. We hope that you will be open to other techniques to produce the desired results that these fluids and other materials are currently producing for you with the assistance and interaction of various industries.

Someday, of course, as on other planets, you will find that you have various technologies and that all of these things can be administered, if you like, on your planet by the very same companies, but it will have no impact to speak of on Mother Earth. It will have an inexhaustible supply of energy, and this energy can be distributed exactly the way you're distributing it right now, if you want—over wires and so on.

It can be distributed to people, and people will pay for that distribution. You can use the system you use right now, if you like, or some other system that you find comfortable.

I'm not trying to corrupt your system. I'm just suggesting that it would be nice if you will be open to that. So an example of a living prayer might be: "I am asking that all industries that are intentionally or unintentionally harming Mother Earth and all people and all beings on Mother Earth be open to utilizing other resources to produce their desired results in a more benevolent way for all beings, including Mother Earth." Do you see? That's a little longer, but we're asking for very specific things.

> *Living Prayer*
> "I am asking that all industries that are intentionally or unintentionally harming Mother Earth and all people and all beings on Mother Earth be open to utilizing other resources to produce their desired results in a more benevolent way for all beings, including Mother Earth."

This is a nice thing that you can say, and it doesn't put anybody down and it doesn't make business a bad thing. It just allows people to be creative in new and wonderful ways and supports that in your system, whatever it may be, in whatever country you are in. Now, this book will be put out initially in English, but someday it will be translated into other languages, and parts of it might be translated before then. So just replace names and so on with the words in your language.

Ask to Clear Pollution in the Atmosphere

Say, "I am asking that the skies above Earth be benevolently and gently nurturing of themselves and are easily able to accommodate other objects within them." That's reality.

> *Living Prayer*
> *"I am asking that the skies above Earth be benevolently and gently nurturing of themselves and are easily able to accommodate other objects within them."*

After all, the tiniest particle of pollution or the largest satellite or space station is an object. We want the skies to feel comfortable with those objects in them, so we're asking the skies to be able to do that.

We're not going to suddenly take a big sweeping palm and say, "Everybody out of the sky now." Quite obviously, we want airplanes and birds to be able to be accommodated comfortably by the skies.

Ask to Clear Pollution in the Water

Say, "I am asking that all water and land that is out of balance through pollution be brought into balance in the most benevolent way by all beings who can help."

> *Living Prayer*
> *"I am asking that all water and land that is out of balance through pollution be brought into balance in the most benevolent way by all beings who can help."*

Ask for Peace on the Planet

You might say, "I am asking that the natural form of peace and love and harmony that is expressed as pure love in its true, natural form be the practice of all beings on Earth now." Now, that sounds a bit mysterious because you don't know what that means, but it essentially means that love—Creator is loving, and therefore, all beings that Creator creates are loving in their true natures—that that true natural love be expressed in the most benevolent way for all beings.

> *Living Prayer*
>
> *"I am asking that the natural form of peace and love and harmony that is expressed as pure love in its true, natural form be the practice of all beings on Earth now."*

Ask to Feel Comfortable with People of Different Cultures

Well, let's do it two ways. We'll do living prayer first: "I am asking that all human beings on this planet find and notice first the common ground, the shared mutual interest and the benevolent characteristics of all other human beings first and foremost."

> *Living Prayer*
>
> *"I am asking that all human beings on this planet find and notice first the common ground, the shared mutual interest and the benevolent characteristics of all other human beings first and foremost."*

Now, in the case of yourself, perhaps you have been raised in such a way that you may not exactly feel comfortable with this group or that group, or perhaps you've had some experience in your life and it has impacted your feelings about this group or that group, and you want that to get more benign for you. Then you might say, "I request that my experience with all human beings be benevolent all the time for me now, in the most benevolent way for me now, and that this have the most benevolent outcome." In this case, you don't say "for me" at the end because it's all beings.

Benevolent Magic

"I request that my experience with all human beings be benevolent all the time for me now, in the most benevolent way for me now, and that this have the most benevolent outcome."

Now, it may sound impossible, but it's benevolent magic and it will be the most benevolent outcome that can be for such a request. Such a statement can easily be supported, you see, by all souls, especially since it will result in the most benevolent outcome. So you don't say "for me" at the end; in that case, it's for everyone.

Ask to Increase Your Spiritual Abilities

Many of you who are reading this book are reading it because you have an interest in spirituality in some form and perhaps you would like to expand your own spiritual capabilities in some benign or benevolent way. In living prayer, you could simply say, "I am asking that my spiritual abilities be increased and supported in the most nurturing and loving way for me now."

> *Living Prayer*
> "I am asking that my spiritual abilities be increased and supported in the most nurturing and loving way for me now."

Or as benevolent magic, you might say, "I request that my spiritual abilities expand benevolently, patiently and lovingly for me now, that I be able to utilize them in benevolent ways for me now, and that they result in the most benevolent outcome."

Granted, you might wind up using your spiritual abilities—whatever they are—for others, but you are asking, so you say, "for me." Nevertheless, at the end you say "the most benevolent outcome"; you don't say

> *"I request that my spiritual abilities expand benevolently, patiently and lovingly for me now, that I be able to utilize them in benevolent ways for me now, and that they result in the most benevolent outcome."*

"for me," even though that's a given because you're asking it and it's benevolent magic. But your spiritual abilities might very well be serving others as well, so the most benevolent outcome serves everyone. And since it's benevolent magic and you're asking all souls to cooperate to bring this about in some form, then that's the way we say it.

I want to be completely clear on this so you understand that when I say "all souls," it includes not only all beings on Earth but all souls everywhere in all creation everywhere. And I assure you that angels are included, that spirits and gods and creators and everyone—they're all included. No one is excluded from that statement. They're not commanded to do anything, but you are just letting them know that this is something you would like now and you are welcoming it.

Welcome the Results

Benevolent magic and living prayer have quite a bit to do with welcoming. Don't say benevolent magic for yourself or living prayer for yourself if you're not prepared to welcome the outcome. No, you may not know what the outcome is. You may be clear, you might say, "Well, I'd like this to work out in a benevolent way," in which case whatever that is, it is going to be the outcome, and obviously you'd welcome that. But other times it might be broader, such as your desire that a disease organism change or mutate, as I said, to something more benign. You may not have any idea what the outcome would be there except that you know it's going to be better.

As the person who says it, you don't have to welcome the disease organism into your life, but you have to be prepared to welcome the results. They might not always be what you think they might be or what you can imagine they might be; they might be better. And maybe you yourself will not see all the results because they might affect others.

But the welcoming aspect is important because it allows what is really going to happen, what is going to take place that will take place in this benevolent way, to have no limits, including the limits of your own imagination or thought. And it can go beyond those limits to develop and deliver a more benevolent outcome than you can even imagine could occur.

In that case, you might have to work on this over time—discover how it works and feel good about it after you have experience. And over time, you might become more welcoming. For those of you who aren't sure what that feels like—or you're sure what it is in thought but you're not sure what it feels like—practice with a friend. Find a friend and welcome her into your home. She comes over sometime; you ask her to come over: "Welcome! Here is your favorite food or drink or something. I got this for you." It doesn't have to be something you like: "I got it for you because you're welcome here." That's a nice feeling.

If you don't have someone like that in your life, then welcome yourself. A lot of you haven't thought of doing this. Walk around in your home or your apartment or your temporary home or apartment or residence (or if you don't have one, wherever you live)—walk around there. Look around. Talk to the objects as if they were alive and even let your hands touch the walls or the chairs if you want to, and just say, "I am welcoming myself here in my home." Even if it's a motel room, it's your home then.

Say, "Welcome to me," or any of those things. Walk around and say it. Don't say, "I feel silly saying this, but I am welcoming me." That may be true, but that doesn't have anything to do with welcoming. Can you imagine going over to your friend's house and your friend says, "I feel silly saying this, but welcome." I don't think you'd feel too welcome. Say what you mean.

This Will Help and Support All Life

I am a Native American, alive in my own time, as I choose to be at this moment of communication through Robert. And having lived on the Earth, I know what it's like to be human. So I'm not speaking from some place in the sky. I know what it's like to be human. I was taught these things by my teachers. We used these words in our own language, and it's designed always to help and support all life.

Over the time of my life, I said thousands of living prayers and did hundreds and hundreds of benevolent magics for all beings. This is very old, and it is my intention in this book to inspire you, the reader, with ancient wisdom as well and to honor you who will go on to do good in the world by saying benevolent magic and living prayer for yourself and all beings.

If there are questions about this in the future, feel free to email Light Technology. Your questions and comments will be used for a follow-up to this book. We might do *Benevolent Magic 2*. Or if you want to write letters, that's fine—probably not phone calls. But we would be very interested to know if you have suggestions or have questions about your particular situation, especially if you think that other people might be in this situation too. And then we will try to answer that in follow-up material in some way, possibly in the *Sedona Journal of Emergence!*, possibly on the website, possibly with another book.

Index

The fundamentals of benevolent magic and living prayer are what you say and how you say it. The following topics refer to examples of the way you might say these blessings.

Benevolent Magic

Shamanic Secrets for Material Mastery

Speaks of Many Truths and Zoosh through Robert Shapiro

This book explores the heart and soul connection between humans and Mother Earth. Through that intimacy, miracles of healing and expanded awareness can flourish. To heal the planet and be healed as well, we can lovingly extend our energy selves out to the mountains and rivers and intimately bond with the Earth. Gestures and vision can activate our hearts to return us to a healthy, caring relationship with the land we live on. Dozens of photographs, maps and drawings assist the process, which cover the Earth's more critical locations.

$^\$19^{95}$ SOFTCOVER 498 P.
ISBN 1-891824-12-0

1-800-450-0985 • www.lighttechnology.com

Shamanic Secrets for Physical Mastery

Speaks of Many Truths and Zoosh through Robert Shapiro

The purpose of this book is to allow you to understand the sacred nature of your own physical body
and some of the magnificent gifts it offers you. When
you work with your physical body in these new
ways, you will discover not only its sacredness, but
how it is compatible with Mother Earth, the animals,
the plants, even the nearby planets, all of which you
now recognize as being sacred
in nature. It is important to
feel the value of yourself
physically before you can
have any lasting physical
impact on the world.

$^\$25^{00}$ SOFTCOVER 544 P.
ISBN 1-891824-29-5

The Explorer Race: Book 1
The Explorer Race
Zoosh and End-Time Historian through Robert Shapiro

You individuals reading this are truly a result of the genetic experiment on Earth. You are beings who uphold the principles of the Explorer Race. The information in this book is designed to show you who you are and give you an evolutionary understanding of your past that will help you now. The key to empowerment in these days is not to know everything about your past, but to know what will help you now. Your number-one function right now is your status of Creator apprentice. The responsibility and the destiny of the Explorer Race is not only to explore but to create.

25^{00} SOFTCOVER 574 P.
ISBN 0-929385-38-1

1-800-450-0985 • www.lighttechnology.com

The Explorer Race: Book 9
The Explorer Race and Jesus

Jesus and others through Robert Shapiro

The core personality of that being known on the Earth as Jesus, along with his students and friends, describes with clarity and love his life and teaching 2000 years ago. He states that his teaching is for all people of all races in all countries. Jesus announces here for the first time that he and two others, Buddha and Mohammed, will return to Earth from their place of being in the near future; and a fourth being, a child already born and now on Earth, will become a teacher and prepare humanity for their return. This book so is heartwarming and interesting, you won't want to put it down.

16^{95} Softcover 354 p.

ISBN 1-891824-14-7

Light Technology
PUBLISHING

1-800-450-0985 • www.lighttechnology.com

The Explorer Race: Book 8
Explorer Race and Isis

Isis through Robert Shapiro

This amazing book has priestess and Shamanic training, Isis's adventures with Explorer Race beings—before Earth and on Earth—and an incredibly expanded explanation of the dynamics of the Explorer Race. Isis is the prototypal loving, nurturing, guiding feminine being, the focus of feminine energy. She has the ability to expand limited thinking without making people with limited beliefs feel uncomfortable. She is a fantastic storyteller, and all of her stories are teaching stories. If you care about who you are, why you are here, where you are going and what life is all about, then pick up this book.

$^{\$}14^{95}$ SOFTCOVER 317 P.

ISBN 1-891824-11-2

LIGHT Technology PUBLISHING

1-800-450-0985 • www.lighttechnology.com

The Explorer Race: Book 12

Techniques for Generating Safety

Create a Safe Life and a Safe World through Robert Shapiro

Wouldn't you like to generate safety—so you could go wherever you need to go, do whatever you need to do—in a benevolent, safe and loving way for yourself? Learn safety as a radiated environment that will allow you to gently take the step into the new timeline, into a benevolent future and away from a negative past.

Part 1:
The Heart Is the Door to the Benevolent Future-Based Timeline

Part 2:
Explorer Race Techniques to Generate Safety and Love

$9⁹⁵ SOFTCOVER 208 P.
ISBN 1-891824-26-0

1-800-450-0985 • www.lighttechnology.com

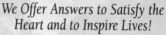